In honour of our precious baby

ABOUT THE AUTHOR

Shaela Mauger and Harpermartin

Born and raised in Wagga Wagga in regional New South Wales, Shaela has pursued her love of graphic design through university and began her career as a designer for a local printer.

Since becoming a mother, Shaela has fine tuned her design passion towards what is now most important to her: loved ones, and cherishing the time we have with them. Now, after half a decade of having her own design business, Shaela has launched Harpermartin — paying homage to her parents' family names — and this series of keepsake books, created to celebrate life and love in all its forms.

The series is available at www.harpermartin.com.au

ISBN 978-0-6482778-0-4

Remembering Me

By Shaela Mauger

Cover watercolour painting by Faenerys
www.faenerys.com

TABLE OF CONTENTS

*"Know you're being guided, by all of us who have survived this impossible hell. You may not hear us, or see us, but we are with you. Beside you. Hand in hand, heart to heart. Always.
Just like your child still is."*

ANGELA MILLER

ABedForMyHeart.com

In memory of Noah

PREFACE

I cannot begin to imagine the indescribable loss you are feeling. I can only wish you comfort in the love that surrounds you, and hope that through filling in this beautiful keepsake book you feel closer to your precious baby.

Every baby deserves to be honoured and cherished. I hope that this book provides you with a way to keep the memory of your baby alive for the many days and years to come. Though they may not be here with you on Earth today, they are forever on your mind and in your heart.

With love,

Shaela xx

Founder, Harpermartin

The date we found out we were having you: _____

What we did to celebrate: _____

_____

_____

Who we shared the news with: _____

_____

_____

_____

OUR FIRST ULTRASOUND

AFFIX PHOTO HERE

MY BEAUTIFUL BABY BELLY

AFFIX PHOTO HERE

THE BABY BELLY

What I loved about being pregnant: _____

_____

_____

_____

_____

AFFIX PHOTO HERE

OUR BEAUTIFUL BABY

_____

The meaning/history of your name: _____

_____

Date: _____   Time: _____

Weight: _____   Length: _____

Hair colour: _____

Eye colour: _____

You looked like your: _____

_____

"Tiny footprints, little toes,
the crinkle of your nose.
No matter how the story goes
You're a dream come true."

JENNY MCGREGOR

jennymcgregor.com.au
From her song 'Memories'

In memory of Jamie

Your Handprints

Your Footprints

PHOTOS & MEMORIES

PHOTOS & MEMORIES

_____

_____

_____

_____

_____

_____

_____

_____

_____

_____

_____

_____

_____

_____

_____

_____

_____

_____

_____

"Can you feel my pain — little butterfly, butterfly
Can you see the sadness — as the tears fall from my eyes
There's a sorrow within me — that's running deeper than the ground
Is that why you came — is that why
Little butterfly."

JENNY MCGREGOR

jennymcgregor.com.au
From her song 'Butterfly'

In memory of Jamie

Where: _____

When: _____

The songs: _____

_____

_____

_____

The people: _____

_____

_____

_____

The service: _____

_____

_____

_____

_____

_____

YOUR RESTING PLACE

"Creating a legacy for a baby as a grieving parent is really no different than being a proud parent to a living child. It is about honoring their relationship with their baby. It is about honoring the part of them that is a parent, grieving and celebrating the little life that changed theirs."

SARAH GARVEY

Carrying To Term
Carryingtoterm.org

In memory of Bridget, Vivian, and Liam

HONOURING YOUR NAME

"These beautiful souls touch down for a moment in time,
but they have such a profound impact on the world around them."

LORI LARSON
In memory of Eva

1ST BIRTHDAY

AFFIX PHOTO HERE

PHOTOS & MEMORIES

a love letter to you

_____

_____

_____

_____

_____

_____

_____

_____

_____

_____

_____

_____

_____

_____

_____

_____

_____

_____

_____

_____

"When I lost my baby, I lost their first Christmas, Easter, birthday. I lost all of the milestones, and hearing them call me Mama. I lost my dreams of our future, and the way I imagined life would be. I didn't know I would miss things that haven't happened, and I never imagined loving someone I've never met, so much."

MEGAN OSBORNE

Aila and Lior
ailaandlior.com

In memory of Aila and Lior

1ST CHRISTMAS

AFFIX PHOTO HERE

PHOTOS & MEMORIES

a love letter to you

25

"Yes, you are still a mother, and you always, always will be.
The love you two share is forever, just as your motherhood is forever.
No one can take that away from you.
Not today, not on Mother's Day, not ever.
You will always be your precious child's mother. Always."

ANGELA MILLER

ABedForMyHeart.com

In memory of Noah

1ST MOTHER'S DAY

AFFIX PHOTO HERE

1ST FATHER'S DAY

AFFIX PHOTO HERE

a love letter to you

a love letter to you

"The same way the sun divides the days, the moment I lost my baby,
my world was split in two:
The time before I carried them, and the woman I was then.
The time forever after, knowing them but not holding them,
and the woman I've become."

MEGAN OSBORNE

Aila and Lior
ailaandlior.com

In memory of Aila and Lior

INTERNATIONAL BEREAVED MOTHER'S DAY

AFFIX PHOTO HERE

_____

_____

_____

_____

_____

_____

_____

_____

PHOTOS & MEMORIES

a love letter to you

"You question why, how, what if, if only. You question it all and probably will for the rest of your life. When you look at their photos and think of their memory... you can't help but think 'what a beautiful question to have'."

MEGAN GAFFNEY
In memory of Ruby Louise Gaffney

YOUR ANNIVERSARY

AFFIX PHOTO HERE

_____

_____

_____

_____

_____

_____

_____

_____

PHOTOS & MEMORIES

a love letter to you

"Easter has found me with a quiet sadness for not setting out eggs to be found, or buying little bunny-eared costumes. I grieve the experiences my baby could have had. I never knew the holidays would bring both joy and pain."

MEGAN OSBORNE

Aila and Lior
ailaandlior.com

In memory of Aila and Lior

1ST EASTER

AFFIX PHOTO HERE

PHOTOS & MEMORIES

a love letter to you

_____

_____

_____

_____

_____

_____

_____

_____

_____

_____

_____

_____

_____

_____

_____

_____

_____

"Holiday dates seem to call me back to my baby, in a new way, with every passing year. I hold their memory dear, always. But it seems these dates in particular, bring them forward to my imagination. Thoughts of how old they would be, and what life would look like with them now. I give myself permission to live in both worlds for a moment, what is and what could have been, and I cherish those moments of grief and joy."

MEGAN OSBORNE

Aila and Lior
ailaandlior.com

In memory of Aila and Lior

OUR FIRST HOLIDAY WITHOUT YOU

AFFIX PHOTO HERE

PHOTOS & MEMORIES

_____

_____

_____

_____

_____

_____

_____

_____

_____

_____

_____

_____

_____

_____

_____

_____

_____

2ND BIRTHDAY

AFFIX PHOTO HERE

_____

_____

_____

_____

_____

_____

_____

_____

a love letter to you

_____

_____

_____

_____

_____

_____

_____

_____

_____

_____

_____

_____

_____

_____

_____

_____

_____

_____

_____

2ND CHRISTMAS

AFFIX PHOTO HERE

_____

_____

_____

_____

_____

_____

_____

_____

3RD BIRTHDAY

AFFIX PHOTO HERE

_____

_____

_____

_____

_____

_____

_____

_____

_____

_____

_____

_____

_____

_____

_____

_____

_____

_____

_____

_____

_____

_____

_____

_____

_____

_____

3RD CHRISTMAS

AFFIX PHOTO HERE

_____

_____

_____

_____

_____

_____

_____

_____

4ᵀᴴ BIRTHDAY

AFFIX PHOTO HERE

5TH BIRTHDAY

AFFIX PHOTO HERE

a love letter to you

6TH BIRTHDAY

AFFIX PHOTO HERE

a love letter to you

7TH BIRTHDAY

AFFIX PHOTO HERE

a love letter to you

_____

8TH BIRTHDAY

AFFIX PHOTO HERE

---

a love letter to you

9TH BIRTHDAY

AFFIX PHOTO HERE

10TH BIRTHDAY

AFFIX PHOTO HERE

a love letter to you

_____

_____

_____

_____

_____

_____

_____

_____

_____

_____

_____

_____

_____

_____

_____

_____

_____

_____

_____

_____

18TH BIRTHDAY

AFFIX PHOTO HERE

a love letter to you

21ST BIRTHDAY

AFFIX PHOTO HERE

"You were, you are and you always will be my baby, and I was, I am, and I always will be your mother."

ANNA M^cRORIE
In memory of Dakota

PREGNANCY AND INFANT LOSS REMEMBRANCE DAY

Honouring your memory

PHOTOS & MEMORIES

a love letter to you

And I would walk a thousand miles,
just to see your smile one last time,
just to see the life in your eyes, reflect in mine.
And I would fight the desert storm,
just to hold you tight and feel your warmth,
just to wake up and see you in the morning, one last time,
because you filled my life, will you fill my life again!

JENNY MCGREGOR

jennymcgregor.com.au
From her song 'Emptiness'

In memory of Jamie

RED NOSE DAY

Honouring your memory

PHOTOS & MEMORIES

a love letter to you

_____

_____

_____

_____

_____

_____

_____

_____

_____

_____

_____

_____

_____

_____

_____

_____

_____

_____

_____

_____

_____

_____

_____

_____

_____

_____

_____

_____

_____

_____

_____

_____

_____

_____

_____

_____

_____

"Tears are words
that need to be written."

PAULO COELHO

"There is no timeline for grieving a loss of this magnitude, so your story always has a place in the world. Share it however, with whomever, whenever you choose."

SARAH GARVEY

Carrying To Term
Carryingtoterm.org

In memory of Bridget, Vivian, and Liam

"There will always be a hole in your heart, the size and shape of your child. Your child is absolutely irreplaceable. Nothing will fill the void your child left. But your heart will grow bigger — beautifully bigger — around the empty space your child left behind.

The love and pain you carry for your precious child will be woven into every thread of your being. It will fuel you to do things you never dreamed you could do."

ANGELA MILLER

ABedForMyHeart.com

In memory of Noah

"Our arms are empty, yet we long for them to be full. We are mothers, but the world often forgets."

ANGELA MILLER

ABedForMyHeart.com

In memory of Noah

"Sure, the intense pain that was present in the beginning has died down to a dull roar. Maybe even a quiet hum. But it's a quiet hum that never goes away. Even in the loudest room, on the happiest occasions, surrounded by the people I love... there is the hum. Even on a good day, behind my biggest smile... there is the hum."

ANN-MAREE IMRIE
anniemauthor.com
Author 'You Could Have Been...'

In memory of Xavier Rocket Imrie

PHOTOS & MEMORIES

PHOTOS & MEMORIES

Big hugs from
www.harpermartin.com.au

CPSIA information can be obtained
at www.ICGtesting.com
Printed in the USA
LVHW072332050220
645690LV00044B/1416